Heroes for Young Readers

Written by Renee Taft Meloche
Illustrated by Bryan Pollard

Adoniram Judson
Amy Carmichael
Betty Greene
Brother Andrew
Cameron Townsend
Corrie ten Boom
C. S. Lewis
David Livingstone
Eric Liddell
George Müller

Gladys Aylward
Hudson Taylor
Jim Elliot
Jonathan Goforth
Loren Cunningham
Lottie Moon
Mary Slessor
Nate Saint
William Carey

Heroes of History for Young Readers

Written by Renee Taft Meloche
Illustrated by Bryan Pollard

Daniel Boone
Clara Barton
George Washington
George Washington Carver
Meriwether Lewis

...and more coming soon

Heroes for Young Readers Activity Guides and audio CDs
are now available! See the back of this book for more information.

For a free catalog of books and materials contact
YWAM Publishing, P.O. Box 55787, Seattle, WA 98155
1-800-922-2143 www.ywampublishing.com

HEROES OF HISTORY FOR YOUNG READERS

DANIEL BOONE

Bravery on the Frontier

Written by Renee Taft Meloche
Illustrated by Bryan Pollard

Emerald Books
LYNNWOOD, WASHINGTON

Daniel Boone: Bravery on the Frontier Text © 2008 by Renee Taft Meloche Illustrations © 2008 by Bryan Pollard
Published by Emerald Books, P.O. Box 635, Lynnwood, WA 98046 ISBN 978-1-932096-61-3 Printed in India. All rights reserved.

A teenage boy named Daniel Boone
    loved roaming through the woods.
He hunted bears and buffalo
    and beavers when he could.

North Carolina, where he lived,
    had rough and rugged land,
and Daniel searched its forests with
    a rifle in his hand.

His family owned a farm where Daniel
    plowed and planted crops.
He always hoped for rain since he
    could hunt when farm work stopped.

He was so good a marksman that
    he always had some meat.
In just one year he killed almost
    one hundred bears to eat.

In seventeen fifty-two he sold
    his bear and beaver skins
to women who would make them into
    hats and moccasins.

He married, had eight children, and
    he longed to move out west,
where few had gone before, to the
    Kentucky wilderness.

Because more settlers moved nearby,
    he wished that he could be
where animals were plentiful
    and land was almost free.

Along with some brave others, Daniel
    and his family went
into Kentucky, naming Boonesborough
    their settlement.

They built a fort to keep them safe
    since they were all aware
that Indians lived on the land
    and might not want them there.

One day, months later, Daniel heard
a scream and leapt from bed.
"The Indians kidnapped three girls.
One's yours!" a woman said.

The teenage girls had been canoeing
but they got too near
the riverbank where Indians
grabbed them when they appeared.

So Daniel, with some others, searched
and soon he found their tracks.
The Indians were far ahead—
there was no turning back.

When Daniel found a trail of bits
of cloth along the ground,
he knew the girls had left this clue
so that they could be found.

Then Daniel saw a cloud of smoke
that rose up in the sky.
*Did this mean that the Indians
had stopped and were close by?*

He crept up on a hill from where
he looked out down below
and realized that they had stopped
to cook some buffalo.

As Daniel scanned the area
 he saw the girls—all three!
They sat together in some woods
 beneath an old oak tree.

Just then he heard a shot, and someone
 screamed aloud in pain
as one of Daniel's men had fired
 at those down by the flame.

As more shots sounded, all the Indians
 soon fled the place.
Then Daniel's daughter ran to him,
 tears streaming down her face.

She hugged him and then told him that
 a big attack was planned.
The Indians would soon swoop down
 and raid their farms and land.

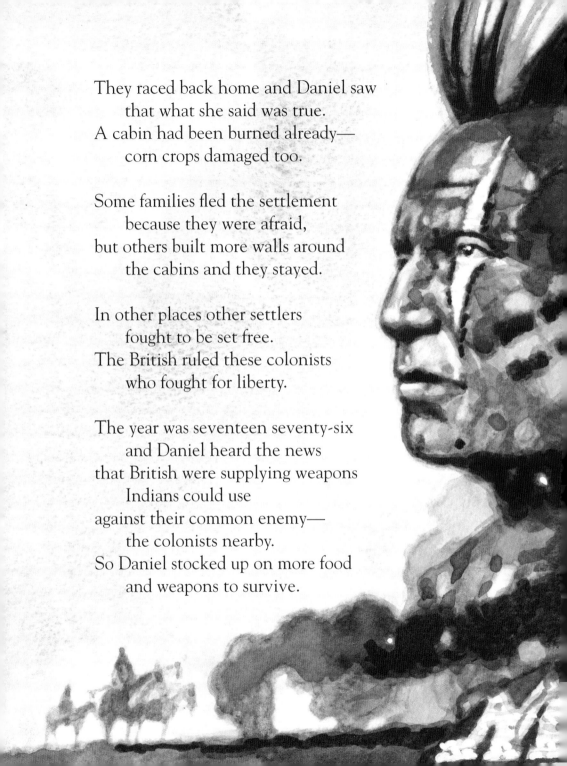

They raced back home and Daniel saw
    that what she said was true.
A cabin had been burned already—
    corn crops damaged too.

Some families fled the settlement
    because they were afraid,
but others built more walls around
    the cabins and they stayed.

In other places other settlers
    fought to be set free.
The British ruled these colonists
    who fought for liberty.

The year was seventeen seventy-six
    and Daniel heard the news
that British were supplying weapons
    Indians could use
against their common enemy—
    the colonists nearby.
So Daniel stocked up on more food
    and weapons to survive.

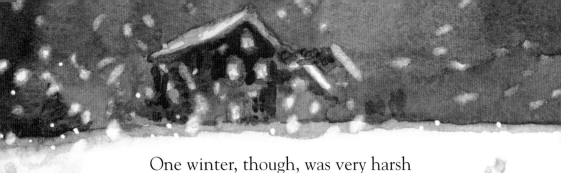

One winter, though, was very harsh
　　and spring crops were quite poor.
Soon food was scarce and gunpowder
　　was used up more and more.

Though Daniel hunted for more food,
　　the meat would not keep long
without preserving it with salt
　　so Daniel, brave and strong,
decided he would venture far
　　to find saltwater springs,
though it was dangerous to leave
　　the fort for anything.

When Daniel found the springs, he filled
　　some kettles he had brought
with water and he lit a fire
　　to make the water hot.

The water soon evaporated.
　　What was left behind
was just pure salt that he scraped out
　　in very little time.

Once Daniel had his salt, he rode
    off on a freezing day
to look for game. He saw a deer
    not very far away.

He silently got off his horse
    and fired and killed the deer.
He skinned it, then he noticed Shawnee
    Indians quite near.

Four men road fast on horseback and
    so Daniel ran and ran.
They chased him as their bullets landed
    close on frozen land.

He knew he must surrender and
    was marched to their campsite.
While there he learned the reason they
    seemed eager for a fight.

Their chief had gone in peace to meet
    white settlers on the land.
They'd killed him and his son, and this
    meant war with the white man.

The Shawnees, to get back at them,
    agreed to set their sights
on Boonesborough, the town they planned
    to crush with one big strike.

First Daniel had to run between
    two lines of Shawnee men
who raised their clubs and tomahawks
    and aimed them right at him!

He dashed and ducked. He zigged and zagged.
    He made it through alive.
With only cuts and bruises, Daniel
    skillfully survived.

The chief then plucked out almost all
    the hair on Daniel's head,
but left a scalp lock on the top
    for him to wear instead.

He decorated Daniel in
    some feathers and some beads.
He dressed him in a loincloth; then
    Chief Blackfish, looking pleased,
sat Daniel down to eat a meal
    of meat, corn, and bear fat.
He told him, "You are now my son,
    a son I now have back."

Though Daniel really liked the chief,
     it did not change one thing—
the Shawnees still planned to attack
     Boonesborough in the spring.

As Daniel learned their language and
     when several months had passed,
he saw an opportunity
     to get away at last.

While on a hunt, as all the men
    chased turkeys after dawn,
brave Daniel jumped up on a horse
    and galloped further on.

And after days of travel, he
    got home; once safely back,
he told his fellow settlers of
    the upcoming attack.

Soon after, Indians appeared,
    and with them Blackfish, too.
An Indian cried out, "Your father
    wants to meet with you."

So Daniel ran to meet the chief
    who warmly greeted him.
The two soon sat together on
    some large soft leather skins.

As tears streamed down the chief's face, he
    asked Daniel curiously,
"You know how much I love you, so
    what made you run from me?"

"I had to see my family," Daniel
　　　said and almost cried.
"If you had asked I would have let
　　　you go," the chief replied.

The chief showed him a letter from
　　　the British, and it said
the settlers must surrender or
　　　great trouble lay ahead.

But Daniel would not do that and
　　　so as they parted ways,
he doubted that their friendship would
　　　survive the coming days.

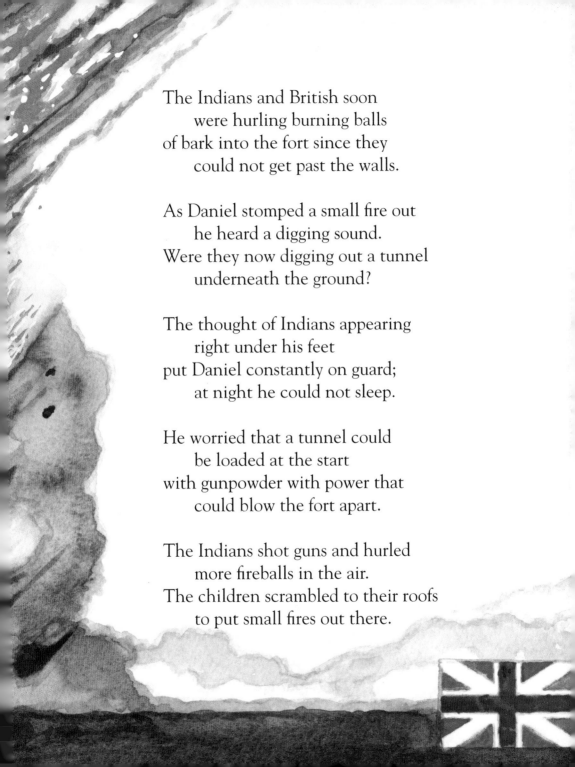

The Indians and British soon
    were hurling burning balls
of bark into the fort since they
    could not get past the walls.

As Daniel stomped a small fire out
    he heard a digging sound.
Were they now digging out a tunnel
    underneath the ground?

The thought of Indians appearing
    right under his feet
put Daniel constantly on guard;
    at night he could not sleep.

He worried that a tunnel could
    be loaded at the start
with gunpowder with power that
    could blow the fort apart.

The Indians shot guns and hurled
    more fireballs in the air.
The children scrambled to their roofs
    to put small fires out there.

Exhausted, hungry, full of fear
    for seven days and nights,
the settlers did their best to try
    to hold the fort and fight.

When everything seemed hopeless and
    looked like they could not win,
the rain began to pour and soon
    the tunnel had caved in!

The rain put out the flames as well,
    and then, surprisingly,
the Shawnee Indians packed up
    and left immediately.

More good news followed afterward
     in seventeen eighty-one,
when British troops surrendered.
     The colonists had won!

These new and young Americans
     now owned land further west
because frontiersman such as Daniel
     went before the rest.

When Daniel learned Chief Blackfish had
     been wounded and had died,
he felt so sad and wished he could
     have been there by his side.

He said, "I'm sorry that I killed
     one Shawnee long ago.
They've been more kind and kept their word
     more than most folks I know."

When Daniel Boone was dying and
        he knew the end was near,
he said, "I tried to do what's right
        while out on the frontier."

At eighty-five years old he died,
        a daring pioneer,
who pushed our country's borders west
        and did it without fear.

Christian Heroes: Then & Now

by Janet and Geoff Benge

Adoniram Judson: Bound for Burma
Amy Carmichael: Rescuer of Precious Gems
Betty Greene: Wings to Serve
Brother Andrew: God's Secret Agent
Cameron Townsend: Good News in Every Language
Clarence Jones: Mr. Radio
Corrie ten Boom: Keeper of the Angels' Den
Count Zinzendorf: Firstfruit
C. S. Lewis: Master Storyteller
C. T. Studd: No Retreat
David Livingstone: Africa's Trailblazer
Eric Liddell: Something Greater Than Gold
Florence Young: Mission Accomplished
George Müller: The Guardian of Bristol's Orphans
Gladys Aylward: The Adventure of a Lifetime
Hudson Taylor: Deep in the Heart of China
Ida Scudder: Healing Bodies, Touching Hearts
Jim Elliot: One Great Purpose
John Wesley: The World His Parish
John Williams: Messenger of Peace
Jonathan Goforth: An Open Door in China
Lillian Trasher: The Greatest Wonder in Egypt
Loren Cunningham: Into All the World
Lottie Moon: Giving Her All for China
Mary Slessor: Forward into Calabar
Nate Saint: On a Wing and a Prayer
Rachel Saint: A Star in the Jungle
Rowland Bingham: Into Africa's Interior
Sundar Singh: Footprints Over the Mountains
Wilfred Grenfell: Fisher of Men
William Booth: Soup, Soap, and Salvation
William Carey: Obliged to Go

Heroes for Young Readers and Heroes of History for Young Readers are based on the Christian Heroes: Then & Now and Heroes of History biographies by Janet and Geoff Benge. Don't miss out on these exciting, true adventures for ages ten and up!

Continued on the next page...

Heroes of History

by Janet and Geoff Benge

Abraham Lincoln: A New Birth of Freedom
Alan Shepard: Higher and Faster
Benjamin Franklin: Live Wire
Christopher Columbus: Across the Ocean Sea
Clara Barton: Courage under Fire
Daniel Boone: Frontiersman
Douglas MacArthur: What Greater Honor
George Washington Carver: From Slave to Scientist
George Washington: True Patriot
Harriet Tubman: Freedombound
John Adams: Independence Forever
John Smith: A Foothold in the New World
Laura Ingalls Wilder: A Storybook Life
Meriwether Lewis: Off the Edge of the Map
Orville Wright: The Flyer
Theodore Roosevelt: An American Original
Thomas Edison: Inspiration and Hard Work
William Penn: Liberty and Justice for All

...and more coming soon. Unit Study Curriculum Guides are also available.

Heroes for Young Readers Activity Guides
Educational and Character-Building Lessons for Children

by Renee Taft Meloche

Heroes for Young Readers Activity Guide for Books 1–4
Gladys Aylward, Eric Liddell, Nate Saint, George Müller

Heroes for Young Readers Activity Guide for Books 5–8
Amy Carmichael, Corrie ten Boom, Mary Slessor, William Carey

Heroes for Young Readers Activity Guide for Books 9–12
Betty Greene, David Livingstone, Adoniram Judson, Hudson Taylor

Heroes for Young Readers Activity Guide for Books 13–16
Jim Elliot, Cameron Townsend, Jonathan Goforth, Lottie Moon

...and more coming soon.

Designed to accompany the vibrant Heroes for Young Readers books, these fun-filled Activity Guides lead young children through a variety of character-building and educational activities. Pick and choose from the activities or follow the included thirteen-week syllabus. An audio CD with book readings, songs, and fun activity tracks is available for each Activity Guide.

For a free catalog of books and materials contact
YWAM Publishing, P.O. Box 55787, Seattle, WA 98155
1-800-922-2143 www.ywampublishing.com